Louie Sharp's

Car Cents

The Essential Owner's Guide
To Saving Thousands On
The Cost Of Owning Wheels

Louie Sharp

Sterling Publishing Group
WWW.STERLINGPUBLISHINGGROUP.COM

Louie Sharp's Car Cents

This is a work of non-fiction. This publication is designed to provide accurate information on the subject matter covered. It is sold with the understanding that the publisher is not engaged in rendering professional services or advice. The information is not intended to replace any legal council or other professional directives. If professional services or advice or other assistance is required, the services of a professional should be sought.

ISBN: 978-0-9845010-4-5

Library of Congress Control: On File With The Publisher

Published by The Sterling Publishing Group, USA | 1.888.689.1130
www.SterlingPublishingGroup.com

Printed in the United States Of America.

Editors: Kathy Eber & Jodi Nicholson
Book Design & Layout: Jodi Nicholson | JodiNicholson.com
Cover Design: Christa Lawrence
Cover Photo: John Brennan

This book may be ordered by calling 847-526-1343
or by visiting: http://www.LouieSharp.com

Transportation / Automotive
Buyer's Guide

DEDICATION

This book was written for everyone who drives, or loves someone who drives.

It is dedicated to the people who inspired me to write it.

First, and most important, is my father who not only taught me to love cars, but how to fix them so many years ago. Dad, I still see your hands when I look at mine.

Next is Bob Kasper, the guy who gave me a chance to talk to the Wauconda High School driver's education classes back when nobody else would let me speak. Thanks for your incredible example. You showed me how powerful and inspiring teaching can be. Enjoy your retirement my friend. You deserve it!

And let's not forget Mike Hansen of State Farm Insurance for joining my speaking team at the high school. You've made our presentation powerful because you never stop sharing your time, talent and wisdom.

God bless you both. My life is so much richer because of the bond we have built as friends in our passionate pursuit of the education and protection of the next generation of drivers. This one's for you.

SPECIAL THANKS

I would also like to thank four people who helped turn my dream of a first book into a reality: Christa Lawrence, for your brilliant creative ideas for my logo and book cover design; Kathy Eber, for all your diligent work editing this project. You always make me laugh; Jodi Nicholson, your input, advice and coaching were so valuable in helping me finish the last lap to bring this project home; and last, but certainly not least, Stacy Sapp for holding me accountable, getting the text on the Lake County Journal blog, and reminding me of everything. You have shown amazing patience with someone who constantly throws crazy stuff at you.

HOW TO GET THE MOST OUT OF THIS BOOK

I want you to take full advantage of all the ways you can save money on your vehicle. By reading this book, you'll be armed with simple and effective action steps you can take immediately so you can begin saving money right now.

Using my worksheets and free access to the website, you can download more documents and information that will assist you in your life long journey to save money on EVERY aspect of your vehicle.

Good luck! I hope you enjoy the ride as much as I love sharing this powerful information with you!

TABLE OF CONTENTS

TABLE OF CONTENTS

LOUIE SHARP'S

¢ar ¢ents

The Essential Owner's Guide
To Saving Thousands On
The Cost Of Owning Wheels

LOUIE SHARP

FORWARD

After over 30 years of experience in automotive repair and 15 plus years speaking to groups about it, it still amazes me when people ask me for my professional advice... and then ignore it. One of the reasons I wrote this book is to share the horror stories I have watched my clients suffer through during my years in business. Thanks to them, I can share what they learned so you can avoid the same mistakes.

You've heard the old adage ...

> *"If you want to be a millionaire,*
> *follow a millionaire around and*
> *do what a millionaire does."*

I love that because it's true, and it also applies to vehicle ownership. There's no reason to reinvent the catastrophe. The information in this book will save you heartache. It will save you lots of money. And it will work every time you apply it.

Success depends on two things: YOU and ACTION! Follow the simple steps in this book and **you will save tens of thousands of dollars** over your lifetime! And if you invest the money you save, you'll be on your way to becoming a millionaire too.

So, take your foot off the brake and stomp on that other pedal. It's time for a road trip!

CHAPTER 1

WHAT TO DO AT THE SCENE
OF AN ACCIDENT,
AND WHY?

A vehicle accident can be a nuisance, a wake-up call, a painful and expensive learning experience, or all of the above. For our purposes we'll define a car accident as any event where damage has been done to your vehicle. It can be something as simple as a door ding from a shopping cart, or as devastating as a head on collision. It can involve property damage, a limb falling through your windshield, flooding or vandalism. It could even be as common as car vs. deer. Whatever the cause, the scene of an accident is where our adventure begins. The steps will always be the same, though they may not all apply in every case.

I've built this guide on all the stories my clients have told me over the last thirty plus years in the collision repair business. I pass it on to you to protect you and your loved ones from the many headaches and heartaches that can follow an accident. I've seen lots of senior citizens lose their freedom because their driving privileges were taken away from them. Having an accident is difficult enough under the best circumstances. By following these simple steps you will minimize the amount of effort it will take to get you and your vehicle safely back on the road.

STEP 1: *"Everyone ok?"*

The first thing to do is make sure that you and your passengers have no physical injuries. Once that's done, check the people in the other vehicle(s) that were involved. If someone is injured, call 911 immediately. Thanks to cell phones, this is much easier than it used to be.

When possible, get everybody off of the roadway to keep them safe from other traffic. Do you have first aid skills or medical training? Use them! If you're concerned about rendering aid, the Good Samaritan law will protect you from exposure to legal action. In my opinion, helping another human being in distress is always better than standing by and doing nothing. The actions you take while waiting for the ambulance can save lives.

STEP 2: *Call the police.*

ALWAYS, always, always call the police at the scene of an accident. No matter how small the accident or damage may seem, it's essential to have it documented by an outside agency--in this case the police. This applies to **every incident**, whether on private property or a public roadway. I can't emphasize this enough.

Check with local law enforcement about the kinds of reports they use in your state. The state of Illinois has two different police reports. One is called an *incident report* and the other an *accident report.* They look exactly the same. The difference is the title and usage. The accident report is used when the incident happens on a public roadway. The incident report is used when the incident happens on private property.

A number of years ago a regular client of my collision shop showed up on my doorstep on Christmas day after his Christmas Eve party left him with a dented vehicle. Uncle George had accidentally hit his car in the driveway when leaving the party, but didn't bother to come in and mention what he'd done.

Whenever you find damage on your vehicle, whether in a parking lot, your driveway or your own garage, call the police immediately.

Oops, that ship sailed.

Ok, so you found yourself in a situation where someone damaged your car, and that same someone talked you out of filing a police report, right? Believe me, you're not alone.

People who are determined to avoid the police can be very persuasive. Ever wonder why? Your first thought was probably *insurance*. We've all heard insurance premiums go up when an accident is our fault. Sounds logical enough. You probably even felt empathy for the driver who seemed desperate to keep this between the two of you. But there are plenty of other reasons why some drivers want to duck the police report. And guess what— none of them are good for you.

Consider these popular reasons:

1.   Driving with no valid license.
2.   Driving without valid insurance.
3.   Driving with previous tickets.
4.   Driving someone else's car.
5.   Stolen car.
6.   Previous accidents.
7.   Trouble with the law.
8.   Illegal alien.

The list goes on, but you see my point. **Not calling the police helps the other driver, not you.** If someone at the scene of the accident is trying to talk you out of calling the police, it is a clear signal that you SHOULD call the police.

This is especially critical when you're not at fault.

"But what if...?"

I know. You're wondering, *"What if it IS my fault and I hit another vehicle?"*

Glad you brought it up. Even if your car hits someone else's car or property, there could be mitigating circumstances that made the accident unavoidable.

To show you what I mean, a friend of mine found herself on a four-lane highway covered in black ice. Several hundred feet before the stop light she slowed to 20 mph. But when it came to actually stopping, it wasn't going to happen. She slid in slow motion into the back of a vintage

Mustang. What's more, the witness was a police officer. The good news for her is that the officer's report explained that conditions made it impossible for anyone to stop, so no fault and no increase in premium. Unfortunately, it did little to cheer up the owner of the (formerly mint condition) Mustang.

Remember, you can avoid paying your deductible when you can document that the accident was NOT your fault. The police report can be your 'get out of paying your deductible' card.

No "buts." Resist the urge to cave in to pressure from the other driver (again). What seems like a quick fix to a fender-bender can cost you dearly when it comes to repairs.

NO MATTER HOW TEMPTING, AVOID THESE TWO ALTERNATIVES TO CALLING THE POLICE ...

1. Driver Information Exchange. Many clients have come into my office after an accident with the personal information of the driver that hit them. The party at fault volunteered his or her contact information promising to pay for the repair in lieu of calling the police and filing a report. But when my clients tried to contact them, they found that none of the information was valid or accurate: false driver's license information, disconnected phone number, false insurance card, and lots more. With no police report to document the accident, my clients had no choice but to pay for the damage themselves, or file a claim with their insurance company.

Potential savings: Your deductible, premium increase, out-of-pocket repairs

2. Hush Money. Some people will try to pay you money at the scene of the accident rather than call the police. This is another bad idea. At the time of this writing the national average cost for a collision repair is $2,300. Personally, I don't know anybody who carries $2,300 in cash in case they have an accident.

My shop recently repaired a one-year-old Toyota Camry with what looked like minor bumper damage. At first glance, even with my years of experience, I would have thought the damage was about $500 to $600. But when we removed the rear bumper cover, we found extensive damage to the rear body panel and lower rear quarter panel. Plastic bumper covers are notorious for taking their shape back and hiding all kinds of damage. The entire repair cost just over $3,800. Had my client accepted the $500 or $600 at the scene of the accident, she would have been short $3,200 for the repair. Thankfully, in this case she had the good sense to call the police right away.

Taking money at the scene of the accident is never a good idea. Rarely will it cover the total cost of the repairs.

Potential savings: Out-of-pocket for the difference between the "hush money" and the actual repair costs.

STEP 3: *Do not move the vehicle ...*
No matter who's yelling at you!

To protect your self at the scene of the accident, it's important to keep the vehicles where they are until the police arrive. I know it's hard when traffic is heavy, and people are honking and screaming at you to move the vehicle. One of my friends keeps her sense of humor by smiling, waving and thanking the shouting honkers.

It may seem hazardous to keep your vehicle where it is. At the very least it's unnerving. We all want to eliminate the angst around us, but be strong. My advice is not to move the vehicle until instructed by the police to do so.

Here's why. Clients have told me that the people who hit them admitted fault and agreed to move their vehicle to clear the roadway. But when the police showed up, these charming citizens denied everything and changed their story altogether. When you keep your vehicle where it landed at the scene of an accident, the police can more easily determine who was at fault and what actually happened. This becomes very important when you have to get the insurance company involved.

If safety becomes an issue because your vehicle is still in the roadway, move yourself and passengers as far away as possible to a safe position until the police arrive. At no time should you move your vehicle until the police give you the go ahead.

STEP 4: *Get a copy of the report. You'll need it.*

Get a copy of the accident or incident report. In my state of Illinois, this is normally done at the scene of the accident. But it can vary from state-to-state, county-to-county and even city-to-city. At a minimum you'll want to find out how to get a copy of the report if one isn't issued at the scene of the accident. This report will have all the important information both you and the insurance company will need to work through the claims process.

STEP 5: *Is it drivable?*

Before leaving the scene, determine if your vehicle is safe to drive. Start by looking for telltale signs of trouble. **If any of these conditions exist, the vehicle is unfit to drive.** Trust me. This is only the short list.

- Fluids leaking from the vehicle
- Any part of the vehicle pushed into a tire
- Bent or damaged rims.
- Any tire with visible damage
- Any deployed airbags
- Seat belt pre-tension devises deployed (If your seat belt pre-tension devise has deployed you will not have seatbelt protection in the event of a second impact.) Not sure? Have the car towed.
- Any dash warning lights that are on since the accident.

- Any broken lights or bulbs (Just as a point of reference, we tow for the local police department. One of the things they pull people over for are lights that are broken or not working.)
- Doors that won't open or close.
- Any kind of suspension or steering damage

The simplest and best rule is **when it doubt, have the vehicle towed.** If you have to ask yourself if the car is safe enough to drive, then it needs to be towed.

When these simple yet effective steps are followed at the scene of any accident, you'll avoid all kinds of problems and save lots of headaches, heartaches and money.

Bonus glove-box card at the back of the book!

At the back of the book in the Appendix you'll find a tear-out sheet to put in your glove box. You can also download a handy card at www.louiesharp.com found in the resource section. The front of the card has the short version of all the information listed in this chapter. On the back of the card are blank lines for you to keep all your pertinent information. I'd like to take credit for this great idea, but it's not mine. I have spent at least 15 years talking to the Wauconda High School Drivers Education classes with the instructor, my dear friend Bob Kasper. This card was Bob's idea. He knows that you will probably be a little rattled at the scene of any accident. This simple little card will keep you out of trouble, and save you from staying up at night memorizing all the steps.

CHAPTER 2

THE WONDERFUL
WORLD OF INSURANCE

Mastering The Basics

Did you ever hear the old joke that asks: *"Do you know what happens when you play a country song backwards? You get your wife, your house, your dog, and your truck back."*

Let's be clear. When it comes to insurance, there is no song you can play backwards that will help you get your premiums back. Regardless of your age, you'll never recoup the money you will pay in car insurance premiums for the rest of your life. Never ever, ever. That's right, you heard me. You could drive for the next fifty years without a single accident, and the insurance company still won't give you any of your money back.

Based on that fact, wouldn't it be a better idea to learn how you can reduce your vehicle insurance premium so you can save money on it for the rest of your life? I think so too. In this chapter that's exactly what we're going to cover. You'll learn how you can save money as often as possible, keep yourself out of trouble, and most importantly, still have the financial security to protect yourself and your assets in the event of an accident.

Decoding The Language

The insurance companies are a lot like doctors. They use a lot of big words and fancy terms. And at the end of the conversation you still aren't sure what they were trying to tell you. Doc, why didn't you just come out and tell me I had a stomach ache? So, to be sure we're on the same page, let's define terms.

Premium is the amount of money you pay for your car insurance monthly, quarterly, semi-annually or annually based on your preference.

Deductible is the amount you pay out of your pocket when you have an accident, IF and only IF, the accident was YOUR fault.

Limits of Liability is the total dollar amount your insurance company will pay for a single claim related to both personal injury and property damage.

Full Coverage Insurance will pay to fix both your vehicle and the other guy's vehicle.

Liability Only Coverage will pay to fix the other guy's vehicle ONLY. It does NOT pay to fix your vehicle.

Uninsured Motorist is a driver with no insurance.

Insured is the person who caused the accident and whose insurance company is paying for all related damages.

Claimant is the person who is the victim of an accident and is not at fault. The Insured's insurance will pay for the claimant's vehicle damages, personal injury - if any occurred, and rental vehicle replacement.

Collision Claim is a claim that is filed when there has been an accident and somebody is at fault.

Comprehensive Claim is a claim that is filed when nobody is at fault. It's often referred to as "an act of God." Some examples of this are vandalism, storm damage, animal impacts (deer hits are the most common), or a tree falling on your car. I think you get the point that these aren't your fault.

The Difference Between Collision Claims and Comprehensive Claims ...

The major difference between a collision claim and a comprehensive claim for you (the car owner) is simple.

Collision claims can have an adverse affect on your driving record and your insurance premium. Almost all insurance companies currently raise your rates after an accident that is your fault.

Comprehensive claims do not have an adverse effect on your driving record or your insurance premium.

I have to stress again the importance of a police report as it relates to insurance claims. For example, let's say you hit a deer on the road. You would file a Comprehensive Claim. To the insurance company, the vehicle damage may look very similar to impact with another car. Without a police report to confirm the details, will the insurance adjuster believe that you hit a deer and not another vehicle? See the difference?

Collision Claim	Comprehensive Claim
Does affect your driving record	Doesn't affect your driving record
Usually raises your premium	Doesn't raise your premium

Loss of Use coverage will pay you for lost income if you use your vehicle for your work/career. For example, if you are a florist and have an accident (either your fault or someone else's) and you can't use your car or van to deliver flowers while it is in the shop being repaired, then the insurance company will reimburse you for the income you are losing because your vehicle is out of commission.

Rental Car Coverage is the dollar amount that the insurance company will pay for a rental car while your car is in the shop being repaired. It's usually broken down by how much the company will pay per day for a replacement vehicle, and for how many days.

Ok that's all great information but how does any of this save me money? Fair enough. Let's get to the meat and potatoes of saving you some money.

Buying Insurance

Here are some questions to ask when buying insurance:

Do I need rental coverage on my insurance policy?

If you don't have an additional vehicle at your disposal, then the short answer is 'yes.' It's still a good idea to do a little research before you purchase rental car coverage. Some repair shops now have free courtesy cars. My company has a fleet of fourteen cars as a convenience for my clients that don't have rental car coverage. To prove my point, a local insurance agent sent out approximately 150 of my free loaner car postcards to her clients to let them know she could save them money on their car insurance by eliminating the need for rental car coverage. Check your area for collision repair shops that offer free loaner or courtesy cars.

While you're at it, I advise you to do some research on the repair shop itself. Make sure the owner is somebody you'd like to do business with before passing up rental car coverage. It won't do you any good to have your vehicle fixed at a shop that offers free loaner cars, but gives you substandard repair quality. We'll cover more about how to find a good repair shop in Chapter 4.

What's the best way to save money on premiums?

The easiest and fastest way to save on your insurance premiums is to raise your deductible. There is an inverse relationship between your insurance premium and your insurance deductible. When your deductible goes up, your premium goes down.

DEUCTIBLE ↑   PREMIUM ↓

When your deductible goes down, your premium goes up. It's just like a teeter-totter.

DEDUCTIBLE ↓   PREMIUM ↑

Currently the most common choices for deductibles are $250, $500, $1,000 and $2,000. The higher you raise your deductible the lower your insurance premium is. Remember the insurance company is NEVER going to give you any of this insurance premium money back. A rule of thumb: *Have 1½ times your deductible readily available.* So if your deductible is $1,000, you should have $1,500 available. The reason for this is very simple. It lets you fix your vehicle for damages that are slightly higher than your deductible. This will keep you from filing a minor claim with your insurance company, preventing the insurance company from raising your insurance premium. This action is actually a double dipper! You will not only prevent your rates from going up, you will also be earning interest on your money when saved in the bank!

Be warned though.
This is tricky territory.

Only raise your deductible if you have AT LEAST that amount of money readily available in a bank account. In other words, if you have a $1,000 deductible, you should have access to at least $1,000, $1,500 is best as I just mentioned. Then in the event you're involved in an accident that's your fault, you'll have the money you need to get your car repaired.

Here's a simple way to calculate potential savings:

Deductible		Payment
$,500 deductible	=	$ X /month
$1,000 deductible	=	$ Y/month
X minus Y	=	Your savings per month

(Note: Your insurance agent will quote X and Y)

Should I use a repair shop that covers my deductible?

The average deductible today is $500. Clients often ask me if I can cover their $500 deductible. My answer is always the same.

"Yes. Just tell me which $500 of the damage you **don't** want me to fix."

Insurance companies work very hard to make sure they don't pay a penny more than what is needed to fix your car. If an auto body or collision shop tells you it can save your deductible, look for another shop. For the shop to save your deductible and still make a profit, it will have to cut corners on the repair. And if the shop does this through an insurance claim, it's called **insurance fraud**.

In fact, any deviation from the repair order that the insurance company writes is insurance fraud. The repair order is a binding contract between the vehicle owner, repair shop and insurance company. If you're doing business with people who are willing to commit insurance fraud, how can you expect them to be honest with you?

Raising your deductible from $500 to $1,000 will literally save you tens of thousands of dollars over the rest of your life as a driver. A mere $1,000 in a bank account drawing interest is a small price to pay for the ongoing rewards you'll get.

Choosing An Insurance Company

How do I choose a good insurance company for me?

Researching insurance companies is a daunting task given all the options available. Here are some guidelines to help you with the job.

- Ask, ask and then ask some more.
- Ask your relatives, neighbors, co-workers and friends who insures them.
- Ask them why they use XYZ.
- Ask them how they found the company.
- Ask them if they have had an accident.
- Ask them how smoothly the claim process went.
- Ask them if the insurance company authorized Original Equipment from the Manufacturer (OEM), aftermarket or used parts.

I hate to be trite, but when shopping for car insurance the old adage is true. You get what you pay for. When gathering information, keep notes and records. The insurance company that comes up with a positive report card the most often is a great place to start looking for your insurance needs.

Visit www.louiesharp.com for resources, special links and current research for insurance company advice and for help with your insurance company search. The higher the company rating is (AAA versus AA), the greater the financial stability it has. That means it can pay claims.

Choosing An Insurance Agent

How do I pick an insurance agent?

Your insurance agent is the voice and face of your insurance company. Since your agent is your direct link to your policy and its servicing, it's a whole heck of a lot better when you like the agent. Unlike insurance companies that can easily be researched online, information on agents isn't as easy to obtain. You can try the Better Business Bureau, but that will only tell you the agents to avoid. Your best shot to achieve that ideal relationship begins again with the people you know and trust.

Ask your friends, relatives, neighbors and coworkers who their insurance agent is. Ask how they found the agent. Ask how long have they been with the agent. Ask how many policies they have with the agent. Ask them if they have experience filing a claim. If so, how happy were they with the process and the results. If you pay close attention to what they're saying (and take notes), one or two names will consistently show up in your area.

After you have a couple of names, call these agents and set up an interview with them. When you meet, be prepared to ask questions about what's important to you, and how they plan to meet your needs. Here are some examples of questions to ask:

- How long have you been in business?
- Are you the owner?

- Are you available after hours if I have an emergency?
- How can I reach you after hours?
- Can you share references from current existing clients?
- Can you handle all my insurance needs?
- Can you save me money if I give you both my home and auto policies?
- What kind of clients are you looking for?
- How does your company handle claims? Is the process different if I am at fault?
- Do you raise your rates after an accident that is my fault? If so, how much and for how long?
- What happens if I have a second and then third claim?

Pardon my detour for just a minute to stress a very important consideration in any kind of relationship. Besides the answers to your questions, what other information are you getting from the people you talk to? How does each person make you feel? Were you comfortable in his presence? Did she look you in the eye? Did he answer your questions directly and quickly? Did she avoid difficult questions or divert your attention to something else? Did he try to sell you things you weren't interested in? If it sounds too good to be true, it usually is.

My point to all these questions is this, trust your instincts.

If the agent comes across as sleazy, then he or she isn't somebody you should be doing business with. After you met with the agent and got your questions answered, did you have a warm fuzzy feeling? If you did, then chances are this is a person you can trust with your business.

The "Not-So-Perfect" Driving Record

Can changing companies improve my premiums if my driving record isn't great?

It's important to note that, unlike most other industries where sharing client information is illegal, the insurance industry can and does share client information on a regular basis. If you're looking to change insurance companies because of your current driving record, be aware that all the other insurance companies have access to your records, and will adjust your new premiums accordingly.

I've been dropped. What should I do?

If your current insurance company drops you because you have too many tickets or accidents, depending on your state's requirements, you'll have to find a company that will provide you coverage in spite of your driving record. In the state of Illinois it is illegal to operate a motor vehicle without insurance. If you're uncertain about your state's requirements, call the Department of Motor Vehicles.

Unfortunately, you'll probably end up having to deal with a substandard insurance company.

You see lots of television ads for companies that provide the minimum required coverage 'on the spot' at rock bottom prices. Be especially wary of companies that can't wait to insure you. These companies have the same access to your driving record as the company that just dropped you. And because they know that you have to buy insurance, they'll charge you a lot more for the same coverage you used to have. They're in the risk business, and you're a higher risk.

What's worse, these substandard insurers will pay only pennies on the dollar should you need to get your vehicle repaired. This is a bad deal all the way around.

As a reputable repair shop owner, I do not repair vehicles for substandard insurance companies unless the vehicle owner agrees to pay the difference out of his pocket. I have found that it's not worth the time or aggravation to try to deal with a company that doesn't care about client service or repair quality. These companies pay approximately 50 cents on the dollar and still expect a quality repair.

Because of the higher risk created by your record, you may have no choice but to use a substandard insurance carrier. It will probably take 3 to 4 years to get yourself back to a place where better insurance carriers are willing to cover you.

Once again, here is another compelling reason to call the police at the scene of an accident. You can see how desperate the other driver might be to keep the accident off his or her record.

Buying Insurance On The Internet

Okay, I admit that I have a pretty strong opinion about this, but the facts create a very strong case to support it. DO NOT buy insurance on the Internet. There are a number of reasons for this. Please keep them in mind when purchasing insurance.

Reason 1: Customer service, or lack thereof

If you want an insurance agent that you can call when you have questions about your policy or to file a claim, don't buy online. It's difficult enough to navigate today's insurance industry because of all the rapid changes. Ten or fifteen years ago you could file a claim and it wouldn't impact your premium negatively. Now your premium almost always goes up if an accident is your fault. Once again I stress the importance of calling the police to keep your driving record clean of accidents that are NOT your fault. This will help keep the cost of your car insurance down!

Reason 2: Inadequate coverage at bargain prices

If you're just shopping for price, you may find yourself underinsured.

In Illinois the state minimums are:
- $20,000 bodily injury per person
- $40,000 bodily injury per accident
- $15,000 property damage

With coverage this low, you could easily be exposing your assets in the event of an accident. In today's market, because of the high price of new vehicles, it's commonplace to have a repair bill in the $20,000-$30,000 price range. You can see that with only $15,000 in property damage coverage you are way underinsured! In this age of lawsuits, somebody is going to be coming after you and your assets to cover the difference between what your insurance company pays and the balance needed to fix their car.

Suffice it to say, if you are underinsured at $15,000 for property damage, you're in even worse shape with $20,000 for bodily injury. Just ask somebody who's taken an ambulance ride from the scene of an accident and spent a day or two in the hospital because of that event. When you are underinsured you are putting everything you own at risk.

No one will ask you the important questions when you shop for the cheapest insurance on the Internet. Nor will they care about keeping you out of trouble or protecting you, your family and your assets.

How often should I review my current coverage with my agent?

I highly recommend you call your agent to review your policy and your limits of liability every year, or after any major change in your assets or circumstances. Do you have enough insurance to protect you and your assets in the event that you are in an accident with both property damage and bodily injury? If your agent can't help you with these questions, maybe you need a new agent. Please refer back to "How to find an insurance agent" and get help. It will give you amazing peace of mind knowing that you and your family are properly protected if you should have an accident.

Why consider Umbrella Insurance Coverage? Is it raining?

Most people are unaware of umbrella coverage. Umbrella coverage is insurance that you can purchase to protect everything you own. For example, you can buy a $1,000,000 umbrella policy to cover your car, your house, your motorcycle, your boat, and on and on and on. It would cost you a lot of money to buy $1,000,000 worth of car insurance coverage. But for a couple hundred dollars a year, you can cover all your assets with a $1,000,000 policy or more.

How much is too much?

You want to be careful that you don't over insure yourself. Estimate your net worth. To get a rough idea, add up what it would cost you to replace all of the things you have in your life that have monetary value. This total should be the amount of your umbrella policy. An umbrella will protect all of your assets in the event you are sued for an accident that was your fault. Umbrella coverage is inexpensive and worth the peace of mind it will give you knowing that you and your family are protected.

When To File A Claim And When Not To File A Claim.

Should I file a claim?

This is the big one--the question that people ask me all the time. The answer is simple. File an insurance claim when it's financially in your favor to do so. What do I mean? By using some simple formulas, you can quickly determine whether or not it makes sense to file a claim. To help you through this process, let's review how deductibles affect your insurance policy, and most importantly, your premium.

Remember, when you have a lower deductible your insurance premium goes up. When you have a higher deductible your insurance premium goes down. So if you raise your deductible you can literally save tens of thousands of dollars during the rest of your life on your car insurance. Of course, doing this means having the amount of your deductible available in an account should you have an accident.

I'd like to take it a step further. I suggest that you have at least one and a half times the amount of your deductible in the bank. For a $1,000 deductible it means having $1,500 in an interest bearing account that you can access easily.

Why? Most insurance companies inspect damage using their own adjusters to make sure that they spend only what's needed to return the vehicle to "pre-loss condition." Period. If you have incurred $1,400 of damage to your vehicle, and have a $500 deductible, the insurance company pays only $900. It doesn't pay $1,900 so that you don't have to pay your deductible. Again, if the accident was NOT your fault, a police report will verify it, and you won't have to pay your deductible. The insurance company will cover the full $1,400.

Here's a simple exercise that illustrates how you can determine the best course of action for your repair.

Let's say you backed out of your garage one day taking the outside door mirror off, and it needs to be replaced. (This is more common than you might think.) The repair estimate to replace the mirror is $750. Your deductible is $500. Would you file a claim for the other $250 to fix your vehicle?

That's an unfair question at this point, because I haven't given you enough information to make an educated decision. Let's work through this so you'll be able to apply it for yourself in the future when the need arises.

Total estimate to repair the vehicle	$750
Deductible amount	-$500
Insurance company will pay	$250

If the accident was your fault, your premium will generally go up for a number of years.

Your annual premium amount	$1,500
(Your agent can get you this)	

Premium increase you will be charged
Your 1st accident (for example 10%) $150 annually
(Again, your agent can get you this)

Number of years this increase
is in effect (for our example 3)   Times 3

Additional premium you will pay
over the next 3 years: 3 x $150 = $450

Option 1
File an Insurance Claim

You pay:
Deductible	$500
Premium increase	$450

Total Paid   **$950**

Option 2
Pay the Repair Bill Yourself

You pay:
Repair cost	$750
Total Paid	**$750**

You Save: **$200**

A quick reference can be found in the Appendix called "Should I File A Claim Calculator".

Are you surprised? A lot of people are when they understand the impact of long term costs. In this case, paying to repair your vehicle out of pocket saves you $200.

The catch is you need to have $750 on hand to pay the bill. This shows you the power of having money in reserve when these types of things happen. But that's a conversation for another day. For today, I just want you to understand that **filing an insurance claim isn't always in your best interest.**

I had a lady come in with $568 worth of damage and a $500 deductible. Despite efforts to convince her otherwise, she insisted on filing an insurance claim to fix her car. What do you think happened? Yep. In the end, the insurance company paid $68 and raised her rates.

I have also seen examples at the other extreme. A client recently used 4 credit cards to pay a $500 deductible. This is especially difficult if the accident has rendered your vehicle unsafe to drive or un-drivable, and you have no choice but to have it fixed to be able to drive anywhere.

There are hundreds and hundreds of stories that illustrate the importance of staying in tune with your deductible and your financial situation. If you have difficulty working through this, and many people do, remember that's why you have an insurance agent. He or she should be able to walk you through this process and help you decide what is in your best interest financially.

Cashing Out

Cashing the check means closing the door

A trend that's becoming more and more popular is taking a check from the insurance company and cashing it before the final estimate is given. Here's how it works. The insurance company issues a check to you before you know the full extent of the damages. It's a gamble, like choosing Door #1 and finding out the big prize was behind Door #3. And similar to a class action law suit, cashing the check eliminates future claims against the agency that issued the check.

Why it's a good idea for you. I got nothin'.

Why it's a bad idea for you.

1) It is incredibly tempting to treat the check as a windfall and spend it on something other than repairing your car. The insurance companies know this. They're playing the odds and betting that you will cash the check. Before 2003 most collision repair checks from the insurance companies were two-party checks made payable to both the owner of the vehicle and the repair shop. The insurance companies stopped this practice and now issue single party checks made out to the vehicle owner only. This gives the owner the ability to cash the check, spend the money on something else and NOT fix the car. Why do they do this?

In 4 words or less—to save themselves money! I have had insurance adjustors tell me they are now trained to write that first estimate 25%-30% less than what is needed to repair the vehicle.

Think about it. If the vehicle owner cashes the check, the insurance company just saved 25%-30% or more on that claim.

What's worse, when you go in to have your vehicle repaired at a later date, you are now left paying not only the check amount, but also the difference for the total repair needed to get your vehicle back to pre-loss condition. This is a rude awakening for claimants that cashed the insurance check and spent the money on something else.

Ultimately, they end up disgruntled because the insurance company that settled the claim has taken advantage of them.

Option 1
Cash the check
Actual repair cost: $10,000

You get: $ 7,000 - 7,500 up front
You pay: $10,000 for the repair

You lose: $ 2,500 - $3,000

Option 2
Cash the check and repair later
Actual repair cost: $2,700

You get: $2,000 up front
You pay: $2,700 for the repair

You lose: $ 700

Insurance companies issue checks like these to make sure THEY, NOT YOU, get a discount. Remember all those premium dollars you've been paying? This is why. Now it's your turn to be paid in full. You're entitled to be made "whole" meaning, *returned to the condition you were in before the accident.*

2) You've just depreciated one of your largest investments faster than usual. A vehicle is the second largest investment most people in this country make. When you cash the insurance check and don't fix your car, you're eventually going to come up short. Let me give you a simple example.

Let's say you have $2,000 worth of damage. You cash the insurance check and spend it on a vacation instead of the car repair. Surprise! Your vehicle has just gone down in value $2,000. In fact, it has probably gone down even more than that, because the insurance company is paying less than what is needed to get your vehicle back to pre-loss condition. (Remember the 25-30%?)

Ok, so you decide to live with the scratches and dents. At some point, though, you are going to get rid of your vehicle and replace it with another one. When you do get rid of it, it will almost always cost you much more than you were paid by the insurance company to have it fixed. If you sell it as is, you'll take a hit on the price you get for your vehicle. As the old saying goes, nobody rides for free. You'll pay the price for not having it repaired with the insurance money when you get rid of your vehicle.

Option 1
Cash the check - don't repair
Actual repair cost: $2,700

You get: $ 2,000 up front
You pay: $ 0 for the repair

When you sell you lose: $ 2,700

---

3) But most important of all is YOUR SAFETY. On average, I'd say that 7 to 8 out of 10 vehicles that I inspect for damage have hidden structural damage and/or lights broken. Driving with structural damage puts you at higher risk if you have another impact, because structural integrity is what protects you and your passengers in an accident.

I recently looked at a damaged 2008 Toyota for a woman. It had been hit in the right rear corner and most of the impact had been to the rear bumper cover. Upon first inspection I would have said the total damage was about $800. But once the vehicle was disassembled, we found extensive structural damage that compromised the safety of the driver. In the end, her total repair bill exceeded $4,000. If she had chosen to spend the check on something other than the repair, she would have put herself and family or friends in jeopardy. What price would you put on that?

Consider too, that if the vehicle has already been compromised by a previous accident, nobody is going to stand behind the warranty in the event of a second accident. Maybe you're thinking the adjuster won't know that some of the damage happened at another time. Believe me, there are lots of ways to distinguish old damage from new damage. At the end of the day, if the safety of you and your family is important to you, then you should have your car repaired instead of cashing the insurance check and spending it on something else.

All three of these reasons should give you plenty of motivation to fix your vehicle instead of "cashing out" of the repair process. You can easily see why having your vehicle repaired by a qualified professional collision shop is in your best interest:

- You don't end up short of money to fix the vehicle properly,
- You protect the value of your second largest investment, and
- Most importantly, you ensure the safety of the vehicle in the event of another accident.

Filing a claim that is your fault will almost always have a negative impact on your insurance premium. When the accident is your fault, the insurance company is going to raise your car insurance premium 95% of the time. Fifteen or twenty years ago this wasn't the case. You might be able to dodge this bullet if you've been with your insurance company for a very long time and haven't had any claims. But in my experience it is rarely the case. Assume any accident that is your fault will increase your payment. You can now see why it is so important to ALWAYS call the police when you have an accident-- especially if the accident _wasn't_ your fault.

More Than One Accident

The scenario gets worse every time you have an accident. My insurance company will raise my premium 10% for three years on a first accident. If I were to have a second accident in that same three-year period, my premium will go up another 30%! Can you guess what would happen if I were to have a third accident in that same 3 year period? The answer is, so long, Louie! They would drop my coverage.

What if you've already struck out?

Now this is where things get ugly. If your state requires car insurance and you've been dropped by your insurance company, what are your options? You have to shop other companies for coverage. When you've been dropped by an insurance company for too many tickets, accidents, or both, then everyone knows it. All the other insurance companies have access to that same information, including your driving record. This makes you a very high risk to all the insurance companies, and they expect to be paid well for taking the risk. You have a couple of choices.

1) Find another quality insurance company that will insure you for a lot more money, or
2) Buy insurance from a substandard insurance company.

A substandard insurance company is a company that insures people that are high risk when they can't get insurance from a quality insurance company.

Dealing with a substandard insurance company has two downsides, and no upside.

Downside #1: You have no leverage. They know you can't get insurance anywhere else and they're going to charge as much as they want to insure you. And they'll get away with it, because they know your driving history and record, and they know that by state law you have to have insurance.

Currently, every state has minimum requirements for auto coverage. They're expressed in three numbers:

$X,000 bodily injury per person
$X,000 bodily injury per accident
$X,000 property damage

At this printing, in Illinois the numbers are $20,000,

$40,000, and $15,000. In Alaska and Maine those numbers jump to $50,000, $100,000 and $25,000. You often see these numbers abbreviated, like fertilizer: Illinois would be 20-40-15. Fertilizer isn't a bad analogy. At this writing, states that require 15-30-10 or less include Arizona, California, Delaware, Florida, Georgia, Louisiana, New Jersey, Nevada, Ohio, Oklahoma and Pennsylvania. What does that mean? If you carry minimum coverage in those states, your coverage is as good as fertilizer.

Downside #2: Your repair quality suffers. In my experience substandard insurers pay just pennies on the dollar to fix your car when you get into an accident. I stopped doing business with them at my collision shop about fifteen years ago. They are impossible to deal with, never return calls and literally pay 50 to 60 cents on the dollar of the cost of a quality repair in today's market.

My point to all of this is that it's very important to know the status of your driving record and the current relationship you have with your insurance company. A couple of foolish mistakes could cost you a lot of time, aggravation and money over a long period of time.

Collision Deductible Versus Comprehensive Deductible

Most insurance companies will allow you to choose the amount of your deductible for both your collision and comprehensive coverage. We talked about the difference between the two. Here's a quick review.

Collision coverage pays to fix your car when it's involved in an accident caused by your vehicle or someone else's.

Comprehensive coverage pays to fix your car in all other incidents; things I like to refer to as "acts of God."

Some examples of a comprehensive claim are: a tree falling on your car, an impact with any kind of animal (deer hits are the most common), vandalism of your vehicle, stone chip damage to the windshield, or flood damage. This is where the police incident report comes in handy. It will give you the proof you need to show the insurance company exactly what happened to your vehicle.

A good insurance company will let you choose one deductible for collision, and a different deductible for comprehensive. This is important for a couple of reasons.

Since a comprehensive claim will not affect your driving record, it will not raise your premium. (If it does, you need to find another insurance company.)

Since you are more likely to use your comprehensive, lower that deductible so you don't have to pay as much at repair time. Also, it isn't tied directly to your premium like your collision deductible is.

So if you get a stone chip in your windshield, and file it as a comprehensive claim, you'll pay a much lower deductible than you would under a collision claim. Contact your agent to ask what your deductible is on your comprehensive and lower it as soon as possible. Then when somebody keys your car in a parking lot it will be a lot less expensive to repair.

What Do You Drive?

Here's something else to consider when you're buying car insurance. There is a direct relationship between the type of vehicle you drive and the cost to insure it. Insurance companies look at a lot of factors when calculating insurance costs including how new your car is, the make and model, where you live, and even the color.

For example, if you live in a large city and drive a new model imported red sports car, you're going to pay a lot more for insurance than somebody who lives in the suburbs or the country and drives a white 4-door sedan. Here's why.

- An imported sports car will be much more expensive to fix in the event of an accident.
- Red cars get 25% more tickets than any other color.
- The chances of having your car stolen or vandalized are a lot greater in a large city than in the suburbs or country.

See my point?

Ask your agent about what affects the rates where you live. This can help you make wiser decisions when you purchase a vehicle in the future. It will also help you save money on your insurance for years to come.

CHAPTER 3

BUYING A VEHICLE

Buying A New Vehicle

Spoiler alert: My advice is to **never buy a new car**. The exception to this rule is if you have over a million dollars in cash and you won't miss the money you spent on it, or anything else for that matter.

For most of us, buying a car is the second largest purchase we make. Yet despite its high cost, it is NOT an asset. It is a liability. An asset is anything you purchase that either goes up in value or makes you money, like a certificate of deposit, or (under normal circumstances) real estate.

A liability is anything that costs you money AND/OR goes down in value. Designer jeans or a cell phone immediately go down in value as soon as you purchase them. So do vehicles. They drop in value as soon as you drive them off the lot. When doing research for this book I was amazed at how fast and for how long a new vehicle drops after it is purchased.

As soon as you drive a new car off the lot, its value drops 20%. I want to be very clear on this--the minute you drive it off the lot...not a week later, a month later or a year later. In 2010 the average car cost was $30,000. If you purchased a new car for $30,000 in 2010, you lost $6,000! It's like taking an hour long drive to enjoy your surround-sound stereo system and new car smell and throwing a $100 bill out the window every 60 seconds.

That's right. $6,000 lost...for what? Was it to impress your friends and neighbors... look cool ...keep up with the Joneses...impress people you don't even know? Each of us has to decide the value of those things for ourselves. Just doesn't seem worth it to me. I would rather keep my $6,000.

Consider these facts when buying a new car. The average depreciation across the country is 20% for each of the first three years. So your car's depreciation doesn't even start to slow down until the 4th year! As you can see by the numbers below the amount of money lost is staggering! Again I will use a $30,000 car.

$30,000 new car cost
- 20% depreciation equals
$24,000 value *as soon as you drive it off the lot*

$24,000 value
- 20% depreciation equals
$19,200 value *after 1 year & 1 day!*

$19,200 value
- 20% depreciation equals
$15,360 value *after 2 years & 1 day!*

You can see in just over two years your fancy new car is worth 50% of what you paid for it. This is how so many people get in trouble with a car loan. You would have to put $6,000 down just so you don't owe more than it's worth. Anything less than $6,000, and you are upside down on your car loan.

Upside down is okay for bats, not loans

When you owe more on your car than what it's worth, you're upside down in a car loan. If you owe $10,000 on your car and it is only worth $8,000, you are upside down on that car loan by $2,000. The price of cars today is higher than ever before. The average vehicle cost in 2010 was around $30,000.

To stay ahead of the depreciating value of the vehicle, you need to put at least 20% down at the time of purchase. Most people don't take the time to figure out the math and at some point get caught in a jam that costs them even more money. If you have to sell your car for any reason, and you're upside down at the time, you can easily lose thousands of dollars.

What if you are in an accident and your vehicle is a total loss? I will talk more about this under collision repair. But for now be aware that if you are upside down in a car loan and the insurance company deems your vehicle a total loss, you will have to come up with the difference to pay off the lien holder BEFORE you can go out and purchase another vehicle.

Many times people are upside down in a car loan because nobody ever shared this information with them. This is why I am so adamant about not buying a new car. I'm not against you having nice things. I just hate to see you weaken your financial situation unnecessarily.

Before I close the topic of buying a new car, let me pass on some general information that you can use. On my website www.louiesharp.com I have some great links to websites that will give you the current value of any vehicle based on year, make, model, options and mileage. I stay current on the dependable resources out there, and have access to the names of some used by major insurance companies to determine the value of a vehicle.

Next, as I was doing research for this chapter, I stumbled across a very interesting statistic. The average American millionaire purchases cars that are two years old. Do you think this is because they know the difference between an asset and a liability? Do you think they also grasp the concept of how fast a new car depreciates? Me too.

If after the previous conversation you still feel you must have a new car, please consider the following questions before you make your purchase. It will help you save more money in the long run.

1. **Discuss the cost of insurance** with your agent before you make your purchase.

2. **How well does it hold its resale value?** Some vehicles hold their value much better than others.

Don't be lazy. Do your homework and find out which one is best for you and your situation.

3. **Can you get it repaired anywhere you want?** Some vehicle manufacturers don't release repair information to non-dealer shops. This means you will have no choice but to go to the dealer to have it repaired, which is often your most expensive repair option.

4. **How readily available are parts?** Some vehicles have slow or non-existent parts supply chains. This can get ugly when you go to get your vehicle repaired and the shop can't get parts. I once had to wait 6 weeks for an oil pan for a vehicle that was in an accident because there was no part for it anywhere in the world. The car manufacturer was at the mercy of the parts supplier. Since the supplier had none in inventory, one had to be made.

5. **What is the cost of maintenance & repairs?** This is very important to consider when purchasing a new car. Does your new car require special fluids? Does it have brand new technology? Have all the bugs been worked out of the system? This list could go on and on.

6. **Don't get emotional.** This is a business transaction. Don't let the pretty little red sports car lure you into making a bad decision based on your emotions instead of common sense.

My point to all this is to do your homework. Make sure you are purchasing the vehicle that fits in your overall budget and expense range, not only on the purchase date, but well into the future.

Leasing A Vehicle

Financially speaking, **leasing a car is worse than buying a new car**. The example I use in my seminars is that it's just like renting an apartment. At the end of the deal, all you're left with is a hand full of receipts.

When you lease a car, you put a small amount of money down and then make payments for a specific amount of time. To give you an example, you could lease a car for $500 down and $250 a month for three years. This sounds okay in theory, because it allows you to get a vehicle that might otherwise be out of your price range. Often the reason people want a vehicle out of their price range is the same reason people buy brand new cars ... for the status symbol.

Here is the low down on this deal. When you lease a car you will never own it. Even as badly as a new car depreciates, you still have some equity in it at the end of the day. Not so with a leased vehicle. You will never have any equity in a leased vehicle.

It gets even uglier when you turn in a leased vehicle with excessive mileage or damage. These types of things can cost you even more money at the end of your lease.

I don't care what your accountant says. Leasing is a bad idea even if you own a company, are self-employed or have other ways of "writing off" the cost. You are better off purchasing the vehicle. You can deduct mileage at the government approved mileage rate, which is 81 cents at the time of this writing, along with all repairs and maintenance. You can also depreciate it as an asset.

Here's one last question. At the end of the lease, where are you? I'll be happy to tell you where you are. You are back at the dealership turning in your leased vehicle. Most people will have not saved any money to purchase a new car. They probably won't have a ride home. Your only option is to lease another car. Before you know it you're caught in a cycle that is very difficult to escape. My advice on leasing is the same as buying a new car. DON'T do it.

Buying A Used Vehicle

It's no longer a secret how I feel about buying a new car or leasing one. Neither is in your best interest. This only leaves one option: purchasing a used car. I know what you're thinking...that you can get a bad deal buying a used car. Sure you can. So I'm going to show you how you can buy a used car and still protect yourself, get a good deal and most importantly save yourself thousands of dollars in the process.

Let's arm you with some valuable information.

1. Check the current value. When you are in the market for a used vehicle, you'll need to know what the vehicle is worth. Visit my site at www.louiesharp.com for access to a great website for determining vehicle values on new or used cars, year, make, model, options and mileage.

Condition is divided into 3 levels - rough, average, and clean - for determining where your vehicle falls. The retail price is what you should expect to pay for the vehicle, or how you should price it if you're selling it outright. These guidelines will keep you from paying too much for a used vehicle. Trust me when I tell you people will sell you a used car for more than it's worth if you are foolish enough not to do your homework.

2. Have the car inspected by a professional. This is where it comes in handy to have a relationship with your mechanical repair shop and your collision repair shop. Most shops will be happy to help you with this task for a small fee. At my shop we do it for our clients at no charge.

Ask the seller if you can take it for a test drive and have your mechanic and collision repair shop look at it. This will help you determine the condition of the vehicle, and prevent most surprises after the purchase is over. If the seller won't let you have the vehicle inspected by your mechanic and collision specialist, you should walk away from the deal. Experience tells me the seller has something to hide if he or she won't let you have someone else inspect the vehicle for you.

Where are the best places to buy used cars? I would suggest the following list:

- Car Dealers
- Fleet Companies
- Rental Car Companies
- Private Owners
- Any company with a fleet of vehicles
- Craig's List
- E-bay
- Road Side
- Trade-in
- Car publications

Car dealers

It's always helpful to have a relationship with somebody at a dealership. Let me detour again for a minute to explain relationships with people in the car industry. You may be lucky enough to have a friend or relative in the business. If you already do, ask them who they would recommend for locating a used car. If you don't have one already, make the effort to develop a relationship with someone at a new and used car dealership. Take the time to develop a relationship with a mechanical repair shop and a collision repair shop too.

I'll give you a great example. I have a client who knows my birthday and those of everyone of my employees. On every birthday she shows up with cupcakes, brownies and other goodies. I can tell you that when she needs anything from my shop, she gets special treatment. ALL of my employees know her by her first name! So if you have a relationship with a new car dealer, give him information on the vehicle you are looking for and he can help you find it.

If the dealer doesn't have the car you're looking for on his lot, he can search for it through his dealer network.

Caution: the pickier you are about specific options, color, etc., the more it will cost you. You'll be better off shopping with the bigger picture in mind. What do you need? *Fuel efficiency, 4-wheel drive, 6-passenger capacity, specific mileage requirements, a convertible ...*

Knowing this will make it easier for the dealer to help you in your search.

There's another reason a dealer can be a great asset for you in your search for a used car. Low mileage cars are often available as dealer demos and rental units that are taken out of service. And when someone buys a new car and decides they don't like it, they trade it back in to the dealer with very low miles on it. You can buy this vehicle at a great savings and still have the manufacturers warranty in place. In fact, most dealers will offer some sort of warranty on low mileage used cars too. As you can see it pays to know somebody at a car dealership when you are in the market for a car.

Fleet Companies

Fleets are a great place to purchase vehicles. In my area there is a large company that purchases new vehicles for its sales people every year. It's possible to get a fair deal on one of these cars. A word of caution though: Make sure the company has the maintenance records to verify that the vehicle was properly maintained under their ownership. When you find a company that takes good care of its vehicles, you'll have a resource for used vehicles for a long time.

Rental Car Companies

Rental car companies are a great source for used vehicles. They can supply you with just about any type of vehicle you're looking for. Again, verify maintenance records. I am often asked by parents where they can find a good used car for their son or daughter. Rental car companies are a great resource for this. Though they often keep cars and trucks for only a couple of years, their high mileage brings their value, and price, down.

Private Owners and Companies with Fleets

Both private owners and companies with a fleet of vehicles are good sources for used vehicles. The same holds true for any company that has a fleet of vehicles. If you pay attention to logos on doors in your area you will soon find these companies. In my area I see cars from a local maid service all the time. Try contacting service companies like them to gather information about purchasing one of their vehicles when they're done with it.

As you can see there are lots of places and ways to purchase a used car.
By following a few guidelines, you can do really well for yourself.

The Top Five are:

#1 Don't get emotional. Base your decision on common sense, not just appearance.

#2 Always have the vehicle checked out. This will save you lots of money and headaches in the long run.

#3 Ask for maintenance records. This will give you valuable vehicle history. If the seller doesn't have those records, there are web sites that do and you can find listings of them. You can visit my site at www.louiesharp.com where I have links to government-sponsored sites and to a number of companies that offer online vehicle history reports for about $30 and up.

#4 Build a relationship with someone in the industry who can help you when the time comes to purchase a vehicle.

#5 Do your homework. Check out vehicle values and you'll see why it's in a car owner's best interest to sell on the open market instead of trading it in. Similar to a pawn shop, a trade-in is valued at wholesale so that the dealer can make a profit when he resells it. If you sell it yourself, you can ask retail.

When you follow these guidelines you will be able to purchase a great used vehicle for a lot less than you would have paid for a new car...and get great value for your dollar!

Remember, be sure to go visit www.louiesharp.com for a comprehensive and up-to-date list of useful resources, downloads and current *Car Cents* updates.

CHAPTER 4

THE CARE AND REPAIR
OF YOUR VEHICLE

Towing

Let's start with towing. Most people don't think about towing until they're stranded on the side of the road. At that point it's too late. As a general rule, vehicles are pretty dependable these days. But life happens. One day you could find yourself stranded for any number of reasons. Do your homework early so you have the answers in case fate springs a surprise test on you.

I consider 2 things when looking for a towing company.

First, is the company reputable? Has it been around for a while? Again ask, ask, ask. Ask people you know if they have ever needed or used a tow company. Ask them who they would recommend if they needed their car towed. Once you find a couple of these companies, call them and compare their rates to be sure you are getting a fair price.

Second, choose a tow company that's close to your repair shop of choice. This will help hold costs down. You may be able to negotiate a better deal through your repair shop. And because most tow companies have a per mile charge, using a nearby tow company will save you money on the mileage.

Be sure to ask about how the company charges mileage. Some companies charge only **"loaded" miles**; miles accrued from the time your vehicle is picked up until it arrives at its destination. Other companies charge **"unloaded" miles**. This adds the miles the tow truck travels getting to the place where it picks up your vehicle. You can run up an expensive tow bill in a big hurry when it is charged by "unloaded" miles.

But hopefully you don't need a tow truck yet. So how can you be ready when you do?

1) Write down all necessary contact information and put it in the glove box of your car.

2) Program the tow company into your cell phone. If you program it in under "Towing," you won't have to remember its name.

Choosing A Mechanical Repair Shop

If you don't currently have a repair shop, how would you go about finding a good one? All together now-- ask, ask, ask! Ask everybody you know who they use. Ask your friends, neighbors, coworkers and relatives why they use that shop. You're gathering information. If the same name keeps popping up, it's a really good indication that it would be a good choice for you. You can also use the internet to research a company. Look for reviews and ratings on how well that shop performs.

Does quality come at a price? I believe there are still many good things that do. If you're looking for the cheapest price for a car repair, chances are you are going to get just that-- a cheap repair. This makes no sense to me. First, because for most people, a car is the second largest investment they'll make. Why would you want to devalue it with cheap repairs? Second, and most important, you put your life and the lives of your family, friends and coworkers in that same vehicle every day. Would you want to be doing 65-70 mph and have to wonder if that cheap repair on your front suspension and steering is good enough?

Please don't miss understand me. I'm not suggesting you spend more than you need to. But there are different grades of repair shops out there. And the cheapest isn't always the best choice for you. This is another place where homework pays.

The BIG Three

There are 3 major types of repair shops: Dealership Service Departments, Franchise/Consolidator Repair Shops and Independent Repair Shops.

The Dealership

Dealer service departments support the vehicles manufactured by the company whose logo is on the big sign up front: Ford, Chevrolet, BMW. Service is the major profit center of the dealership. The days of large profit margins through car sales are over.

Even financing is often handled by an outside company. Since the overhead needed to support new and used car sales is huge, these folks have to make their money on the back end--service and repair.

That's why the labor rate at a dealership is usually 20% to 40% higher than at a franchise or an independent shop.

The Franchise/Consolidator

The franchise/consolidator usually has a national brand name tied to it. A good example of this is Aamco Transmissions. The overhead and labor rates in these shops aren't as high as a dealership. But these guys pay a franchise fee that funds national advertising which still makes them higher than independent shops.

The Independent

The third type of shop is usually owned and managed by an entrepreneur. These independents don't have to support a location big enough to store and sell cars. They don't have to pay franchise fees for national advertising campaigns. Their overhead is tied only to their direct cost of doing business. It's no wonder that 'ABC Garage' has the lowest rates of the three types of shops.

Warranty Wisdom

Ok, I already know what you're thinking. "If I have my vehicle repaired anywhere other than the dealer, it will void the warranty." Nothing could be further from the truth. Yet thanks to a great advertising campaign from car manufacturers and car dealers, lots of people believe it.

In 1975 Congress passed the Magnuson-Moss Act which allows you to have your car repaired and maintained anywhere you choose without it affecting the manufacturer's warranty.

Contrary to popular belief, the dealership is not the only — and certainly not the best — place to get an oil change.

Quick-Change Oil Companies

While we're here, I want to weigh in on quick-change oil companies. When I owned my mechanical repair shop one of my best referral sources was the local quick-change oil company. There were many reasons for this, and all of them are the same reasons you don't want to use a quick-change oil service.

Reason #1 It's very difficult to make money just changing oil, especially at their give-away pricing. So to make real money, they try to "up-sell" you something. Have you ever noticed how many things your car seems to need when you take it in for a quick oil change? You're told you need wipers, air filter, fluid changes and more. That's because they need to sell you more than an oil change to make a good profit.

Reason #2 90% of the time the person changing your oil is a young person who only knows how to change your oil. What's wrong with this picture? This newbie doesn't have the experience or knowledge to diagnose and inspect your vehicle for the repairs your car might truly need.

Reason #3 And this is very important. Most quick-change oil companies use what is called a "pit" to change your oil. The way this works is the vehicle is driven over a hole in the floor and the person changing your oil walks into the pit under the vehicle to do the work. The problem is, the vehicle is never lifted off the ground. When all the weight of the vehicle is still on the suspension it's impossible to accurately inspect your ball joints, tie rod ends and steering linkage, to name just a few, for wear and/or damage.

To illustrate, my neighbor regularly got her oil changed by someone who did it cheaper than my shop. One day she called and told me something seemed to be wrong with the front end of her car. After inspecting the vehicle, we discovered she needed over $1,200 worth of front suspension work. I was certain that the wear and tear on her front end didn't happen overnight. It happened over time because the vehicle was never put up on a rack when the oil was changed.

When the first ball joint starts to get loose and wear, it puts more strain on other parts. Then those damaged parts affect other parts. The process starts to snowball and before you know it you need thousands of dollars in repairs.

Keeping up with regular maintenance

I cannot overstress the importance of regularly scheduled maintenance to prolong the life and safety of your vehicle. Why would you not protect your second largest investment with regularly scheduled maintenance? A good analogy for this is your body. If you ignore and abuse your body for 50 years you shouldn't be surprised if you have health problems. Your vehicle is no different. Run it for 50,000 miles with no regard for care and maintenance and it's bound to give you problems too.

I highly recommend that you have regularly scheduled maintenance done to your vehicle. If you've done your leg work, you've already found a reputable, fair and dependable shop you can trust and count on. It will have access to the same recommended maintenance that the manufacturer provided you. Good repair shops will put you on a program to track this for you. Take advantage of it. It's in your best interest.

Regularly scheduled maintenance will save you lots of money on vehicle repairs in the long run. Much like your body, your car gives you early warning signs. Getting these signs diagnosed and handled as soon as possible prevents them from getting worse. When you ignore symptoms of trouble, you will always pay more money in the end. Like tooth decay, these problems won't heal themselves. Left unattended they will compound your problems, by adding cost and compromising the safety of you and your loved ones. For the safety of everybody concerned and to prevent higher repair costs, keep your vehicle maintained with regularly scheduled check-ups.

Parts

There are now a wide variety of parts to choose from when having your car repaired. I'll break them down by category so you can see how they apply to both mechanical repairs and collision repair.

OEM: Original Equipment from the Manufacturer

OEM parts are available from the company that manufactured your vehicle. Normally these parts are purchased from a car dealership that carries parts for your make of vehicle. For example, you buy Chevy, Olds, Cadillac and GMC parts from a GM dealer.

Collision repair with OEM parts Pros & Cons:

Pros:
1. Sheet metal parts fit better
2. Sheet metal parts meet safety standards
3. Electrical parts match wiring plugs
4. Electrical parts match voltage exactly

Cons:
1. Sometimes these parts are the most expensive
2. Parts often delayed from low inventories

Mechanical repair with OEM parts Pros & Cons:

Pros:

1. Will always match for fit and form
2. Wiring plugs match
3. Correct voltages
4. Easy to diagnose problems

Cons:

1. More expensive than other options
2. Parts often delayed from low inventories

From a repair stand point, OEM parts are usually the easiest and fastest to use. But if you're paying for the repairs out of your pocket, they may not be the most cost-effective. In recent years OEM parts have seen some huge price increases on parts that aftermarket companies aren't able to produce cost-effectively.

Rebuilt or Remanufactured Parts

There are lots of companies in the market place who are rebuilding or remanufacturing OEM parts. Some specialize in rebuilt parts like starters, alternators and a variety of other electrical components. Some remanufacture (repair OEM damaged parts) plastic bumper covers, aluminum rims, wiring harnesses, radiators and this list goes on. These parts are normally of very good quality and often a less expensive alternative to OEM parts. They usually come with a warranty so you can have some confidence in their quality.

Collision repair with rebuilt or remanufactured parts Pros & Cons:

Pros:

1. They are less expensive
2. They fit well
3. They maintain the safety standards of the vehicle
4. They are usually readily available

Cons:

1. If a low quality company is used, parts are not as good.
2. Parts aren't always delivered correctly the first time

Mechanical repairs with rebuilt or remanufactured parts Pros & Cons:

Pros:

1. Cost effective
2. Match and maintain electrical standards
3. Readily available

Cons:

1. Warranty may not match OEM
2. If a low quality company is used, parts are not as good.

Aftermarket Parts:

Aftermarket parts are parts that have been made by companies other than those provided from the manufacturer. Let's use General Motors as an example. GM doesn't make all the parts for the vehicles they build; they may use A/C Delco for the starters or alternators on their vehicles. A starter or alternator that is made by ANY company other than A/C Delco would be considered an aftermarket part. It's important to know this, because the part may not have the exact same voltage or amperage output. It may have a different plug or wiring harness. And these parts often don't carry the same warranty.

After market sheet metal parts (hoods, fenders, doors etc.) are created differently. They must be "reverse engineered" because the automobile manufacturer doesn't share the dimensions, exact type of metal used, or the amount of metal including thickness and density. An aftermarket supplier will purchase a fender, measure it, and try to reproduce it from these measurements.

You may have already figured out this isn't the best way to produce parts. There's lots of room for error, especially when measuring curved or rounded surfaces. It is almost impossible to determine the correct metal content and the exact weight of the part.

These parts rarely fit correctly or give you the same protection as OEM parts.

Collision repair with after-market parts Pros & Cons:

Pros:
1. These parts are less expensive
2. These parts are usually easily available

Cons:
1. Parts normally don't meet manufacturers standards
2. Parts normally don't fit or perform as well
3. Parts may diminish the value of your vehicle.

Choosing A Collision Repair Shop (Body Shop)

If you don't currently have a collision repair shop, how would you go about finding a good one? All together now-- ask, ask, ask! Ask everybody you know who they use. Ask your friends, neighbors, coworkers and relatives why they use that shop. You're gathering information. If the same name keeps popping up, it's a really good indication that it would be a good choice for you. You can also use the internet to research a company. Look for reviews and ratings on how well that shop performs.

Does quality come at a price? I believe there are still many good things that do. If you're looking for the cheapest price for a car repair, chances are you are going to get just that-- a cheap repair. This makes no sense to me. First, because for most people, a car is the second largest investment they'll make. Why would you want to devalue it with cheap repairs? Second, and most important, you put your life and the lives of your family, friends and coworkers in that same vehicle every day. Would you want to be doing 65-70 mph and have to wonder if that cheap repair on your front suspension and steering is good enough?

Please don't miss understand me. I'm not suggesting you spend more than you need to. But there are different grades of repair shops out there. And the cheapest isn't always the best choice for you. This is another place where homework pays.

Wait a minute! I already read this!

If the last 3 paragraphs sound familiar, it's because they are almost identical to the paragraphs on how to find a mechanical repair shop. We don't need to re-invent the wheel every time we try to do something. If it works and gets you the results you want, just repeat it and you will succeed every time, just like a recipe!

So let's get started with the portion of this book that is truly nearest and dearest to my heart, collision repair. There are many places we could start this conversation. I say we should cover the most volatile part first:

Who picks the repair shop—you or the insurance company?

Insurance companies naturally want to steer you to a shop where they have a contractual relationship. This contract usually gives discounts and concessions to the insurance company to hold the cost of the repair down. In return, the shop gets a steady stream of work. These mutually beneficial business agreements are called Direct Repair Programs or DRPs. The majority of DRP contracts give the insurance company a discount on the cost of the collision repair.

These discounts can include but aren't limited to:

1. Labor rate discounts
2. Parts price discounts
3. Paint and Material Discounts and/or P&M caps
4. Rental Car discounts
5. Storage fee discounts
6. Total loss discounts
7. Guaranteed cycle time (Cycle time is the time it takes to complete the repair)

The insurance companies are very good at "steering" or persuading people to use their DRP shops. Because of the discounts, it's obvious why insurance companies are motivated to do this. But here's what they don't tell you:

YOU HAVE THE RIGHT TO GET YOUR VEHICLE REPAIRED AT THE COLLISION REPAIR SHOP OF _YOUR_ CHOICE!

Here's what you need to know about these DRP programs:

1. By LAW you have the right to have your vehicle repaired wherever YOU want.

2. It is illegal for any insurance company to "steer" you, tell you, or persuade to use a specific collision repair shop.

3. These discounts may compromise the quality of the repair done to your vehicle. The average profit a collision repair shop in America is 10%. The discounts with some DRP programs are so large that some make little or no money. In some cases the collision shop loses money on the repair. Let me help you understand this concept. If a collision repair shop has 10 cars to fix and one of them is a "DRP" discounted repair, which job do you think the shop will rush and cut corners on to make money? Exactly.

4. You spend years paying insurance premiums. Now it's the insurance company's turn to pay up. You deserve a quality repair, not the cheapest repair. As I stated earlier, quality still has a price in automotive repair.

5. You and the shop may lose your right to choose the best parts possible for your repair.

6. Insurance companies are selective about the shops they choose. This isn't a completely bad idea. There are still some collision repair shops out there that shouldn't be fixing vehicles because they don't have the proper training or the right equipment to do it correctly. Then again, the other half of this story is there are a lot of shops that are qualified and meet

all the insurance company requirements and criteria, but aren't allowed to participate in the DRP programs because of guidelines that the insurance companies create. The result is that quality collision shops are excluded from the insurance company's list of "approved providers." This gives the consumer the impression that any shop NOT on the list is not a quality shop when in fact, it might be a much better choice. Many quality shops are losing repairs because the insurance company has chosen not to include them on its list of "approved providers".

7. Quality repair shops can still do your collision repairs even if they are not on the insurance company's "approved provider" list. Most will do the repairs with no additional cost to you other than your deductible if it applies.

8. Insurance companies do NOT warranty any collision repairs. Some of the advertising on TV and radio are full of flat out lies. The warranty on all collision repairs always falls on the repair shop. If you have a problem with your vehicle after a repair is completed and you call the insurance company, they'll send you back to the shop that did the repairs.

9. In some instances the quality of customer service drops. The main reason for this is that the collision shop didn't have to work very hard to capture you as a client, because the insurance company sent

them and they don't place a high value on your business.

Why would anyone be a DRP shop?

You may be asking why a body shop or a collision shop would participate in an insurance company's Direct Repair Program. Well, there are a couple of reasons.

First, most of these business owners aren't financially savvy enough to run their business as profitably as possible. As of this writing the average net profit for a collision shop (after all the bills are paid) is 8%-12%. If the shop is giving the insurance company a 5% discount they are giving up approximately 50% of their profit. Many believe that the DRP program is a good deal because they don't know the real truth.

The second reason shops stay in these programs is it is the path of least resistance. The insurance company does all the work to send them clients with cars to fix. The down side of this for the vehicle owner is he is not as valued by the collision shop because they didn't have to do any work to capture you as a client.

When a business does the necessary work to win new clients, they view them completely differently than clients that were given to them. This is true for all of us. Remember how hard you worked and saved to buy your first new car? Do you remember how well you took care of it?

One last point I would like to make is that these DRP shops are making their relationship with the insurance company more important than the quality of their repairs and client service. At one time my shop was involved in a DRP program with a major insurer in my area. When the insurance company decided to change its program and asked for concessions (discounts), I chose to not participate. Instead I got busy educating my clients. Today I do more work than ever before for this insurance company without giving them a discount.

Don't get me wrong. Not all DRP's are bad. There are some insurance companies that still care about a quality repair and, more importantly, client service. These insurance companies aren't asking for discounts or concessions. They are expecting a quality repair in a timely fashion with outstanding customer service. In my opinion this is a winning combination for all parties involved: the consumer, the insurance company and the collision repair shop.

Consolidators

Like chain stores, consolidators are collision repair shops that have a number of different locations: sometimes many locations in a single state, or lots of locations across a number of states. Consolidators normally have relationships with insurance companies. For your own protection it's important that you understand how consolidators work.

Quality?

For consolidators, profit is a numbers game. They work on the premise that they can make more money by fixing wrecked cars as fast and as cheaply as possible. Most of them believe that by giving the insurance companies cheaper rates and discounts they can make up the difference by fixing more vehicles. This is certainly not the best scenario for your vehicle repair.

In the real world it will always take a certain amount of time to fix $3,000 worth of damage. If prices are discounted and production accelerated, something has to give. It will almost always be quality. To make a profit at a discounted price and still stay in business, a company has to cut corners.

In the collision repair industry the national average net profit is between 8% and 12%. That means if a shop does a $1000 repair, the total amount of money left over, net profit, is between $80 to $120. Add discounts on parts and labor for the insurance company, and there isn't going to be very much money left over for profit. To overcome these discounts AND make money a shop has to look for ways to cut corners. This is how quality suffers.

Customer service

Another issue with consolidators is communication. You won't ever come in contact with the owner. Instead you'll be dealing with corporate employees. Remember how consolidators look for ways to cut corners? One way is not to pay their employees what they're worth for their skills and experience. Underpaid employees who don't own the company will probably not be as committed to quality and client satisfaction as an employee who is well compensated. This is how customer service starts to suffer.

To be fair, not all consolidators are bad. But I would advise you to be very cautious when dealing with them.

CHAPTER 5

TO TOTAL
OR NOT TO TOTAL

I am often asked what a *total loss* is. A total loss is a phrase used to describe a vehicle that has incurred more damage than the value of the vehicle at the TIME of the accident. In other words, if your vehicle is *currently* valued at $10,000 has an accident, and the repairs to fix it would be $11,000, the vehicle is deemed a total loss. To be clear, the amount you initially paid for the vehicle does not come into play because the vehicle has depreciated in value. (If this Is unclear then please refer to Chapter 3 - Buying a Car.)

It makes no sense to spend $11,000 to fix a vehicle that is currently only worth $10,000. It gets a little trickier with insurance payments. Most insurance companies use 70% to 80% of their initial estimate to deem a vehicle a total loss. So using our example, if your vehicle is valued at $10,000, and the initial estimate is $8,000, the insurance company will deem it a total loss knowing that with the extra 20-30%, the repair will exceed the current value of the car.. Insurance companies don't want to pay more than a vehicle is worth to fix it. It doesn't make good business sense. They would rather pay you $10,000 for your car than pay a repair shop $11,000 to fix it.

If there's a question about whether or not a car can be fixed, it's a good idea to do a complete disassembly to access all the damage and determine if the vehicle is a total loss. In cases where visual inspection of the vehicle's age and condition make an obvious total loss, no disassembly is needed.

When the vehicle condition is borderline, people often ask me if they should repair or total it. There are a couple of things to take in to consideration when this is the case. First, let's be clear. I'm talking about a vehicle that would need complete disassembly and repair bill of $8,000 on a vehicle worth $10,000. The answer is, it depends on your situation.

If you own the vehicle free and clear with no outstanding debt and have the ability to purchase another vehicle, then it's probably in your best interest to have it totaled. If you owe a fair amount of money on the vehicle without the ability to pay it off and purchase another vehicle then it is best for you to have the vehicle repaired.

Here is where it helps to have a working, trusting relationship with your collision repair shop. The collision shop can help negotiate with the insurance company to get the best result for you based on your financial situation.

Let's play our example out visually on the next few pages.

Scenario 1

Vehicle value	$10,000
Repair estimate	$ 8,000
Balance owed on it	$ 0

Have down payment? Yes

TOTAL THE VEHICLE
You'll have:
Money from insurance $10,000

Scenario 2

Vehicle value	$10,000
Repair estimate	$ 8,000
Balance owed on it	$ 7,000

Down payment money? No

TOTAL THE VEHICLE

You'll get	$10,000
You owe	- 7,000
You'll have	$ 3,000
	and no vehicle

Scenario 3

Vehicle value $10,000
Repair estimate $ 8,000
Balance owed on it $ 7,000
Down payment money? No

FIX THE VEHICLE
You'll still have
a vehicle worth $10,000

If your vehicle is worth $10,000 and you still owe $7,000 on it, after the $8,000 repair to pre-loss condition and eventual payoff of the loan, you would have $1,000 left. If you have no money in the bank, then it's in your best interest to have the vehicle repaired. You simply can't replace an $8,000 vehicle with a $1,000.

I would again like to stress how important it is NOT to be upside down in a car loan especially when you have an accident that makes your vehicle a total loss. A client of mine bought a fancy new vehicle with all the extras, custom sports package, power everything, fancy ground effects and sunroof. She ran the car off the road hit a metal culvert and rolled the car end over end. Fortunately she wasn't hurt. But the vehicle was a total loss.

Unfortunately, the client owed $18,000 on a vehicle that was currently valued at $15,000. The insurance company paid her $15,000. And she was left with a $3,000 loan balance, no car to drive and no money in the bank. She was in tears with no way to get to work. I have seen too many of these kinds of events to count. Be aware of your vehicle's value and how much you still owe on it. It can make all the difference. It also underscores the importance and power of saving your money.

Damaged forever? No way. While we're at it, let's clear up an old wives tale.

Have you heard someone say that once a vehicle is in an accident it is never the same? **Not true.** I agree that there are still some repair shops that don't have the qualifications, training and equipment to do quality repairs. But when you use a reputable shop, you get a **quality repair** with a **lifetime warranty**.

The wives tale persists based on the misconception that the collision repair industry is way behind when it comes to computers, technology and innovation. **Again, not true.** I could go on for pages about how advanced the collision repair industry is today. In the three decades I've been in the industry it has come light years from where it was when I first started. Dealing with a quality shop makes all the difference.

Use the handy calculator located at the back of the book on page 98 in the Appendix to determine whether or not to total your damaged car. You may also visit www.louiesharp.com to download a full version of the *Should I File A Claim Calculator.*

CHAPTER 6

KNOW YOUR RIGHTS

Your Rights As A Vehicle Owner

1. You have the right to a police report.
2. You have the right to use the towing company of your choice.
3. You can not be charged more than $100 over the repair estimate without your prior approval in the state of Illinois.
4. You have the right to use the body shop/collision repair shop of your choice. It is against the law for an insurance company to "steer" you to their repair shop.
5. You have the right to know exactly what is going to be done to your vehicle on any repairs.
6. You have the right to have a vehicle inspected before you purchase it. This includes an inspection by both a certified mechanic and collision shop.
7. You have the right to inspect, check and test drive your vehicle before you pay for any repairs.
8. You have the right to ask about the warranty on any type of repairs before you approve them.
9. You - and only you - have the right to authorize repairs on your vehicle.
10. You have the right to check the value of any vehicle before you purchase it.

CHAPTER 7

FUEL FACTS

Gas Saving Tips

1. Avoid prolonged warming up of the engine even on cold mornings. 30 to 45 seconds is plenty.

2. Avoid "revving" the engine. This wastes fuel needlessly.

3. Eliminate jack-rabbit starts. Accelerate slowly when starting from a dead stop. Don't push the pedal down more than ¼ of the total foot travel. This allows for peak fuel efficiency.

4. Buy gas at the coolest part of the day. (see gas pumping tips)

5. Choose type and brand of gas carefully. Certain brands will provide you with greater economy because of better quality.

6. Avoid overfilling the tank to the top. Overfilling results in gas sloshing over and out of the tank.

7. Drive steadily. Slowing down and speeding up wastes fuel. Avoid tailgating – the driver in front of you is

unpredictable. Not only is it unsafe, but your economy is affected when they slow down unexpectedly.

8. When approaching hills, accelerate before the hill not on it.

9. Avoid rough roads whenever possible, because dirt or gravel will rob you of up to 30% of your gas mileage.

10. Use alternate roads when safer, shorter and straighter. Compare traveling distance differences, and remember that corners, curves and lane jumping requires extra gas. The shortest distance between 2 points is always a straight line.

11. Stoplights are usually timed for your motoring advantage. By traveling at the legal speed limit you increase your chances of hitting more green lights along the way.

12. Avoiding backing up saves gas. If possible park your car or truck to avoid backing up.

13. Regular tune-ups ensure the best gas mileage.

14. Remove all excess weight from your vehicle. The more weight you are moving around, the more fuel is needed to move it.

15. Car pool. This is a great way to have fun and have other riders chip in to help pay for gas!

16. Combine errands in the same trip.

17. When it's time for a new car, downsize! Newer cars are more fuel efficient and roomier!

18. Avoid driving when you can. Take the train, the bus, carpool, your bike or walk. All of them will save you money and wear and tear on your vehicle. Some of them will even improve your health!

19. It's a drag, man ...

- Keep windows closed when traveling at highway speeds. Open windows cause air drag and reduce your mileage by as much as 10%.

- Don't let your left foot rest on the brake pedal, even the slightest pressure will create drag.

- Inspect wheel alignment and suspension parts for uneven wear which creates engine drag.

- Inflate all your tires to the maximum limit. Inflated tires roll easier reducing drag.

- During cold weather remove ice and snow from the undercarriage. It adds additional weight and increases wind drag.

- Don't add bigger or wider tires. This may look good, but it increases drag too.

Gas Pumping Tips For Fuel Savings

1. Only buy or fill up your car or truck early in the morning when the ground temperature is still cold. Remember that all service stations have their storage tanks buried below ground. The colder the ground the more dense the gasoline. When it gets warmer, gasoline expands. So if you buy in the afternoon or evening...your gallon is not a gallon. The specific gravity and the temperature of gasoline play an important role in how much you get.

2. When you are filling up, do not squeeze the trigger of the nozzle to a fast mode. If you look you will see that the trigger has three (3) stages: low, middle, and high. You should be pumping in the low mode, thereby minimizing vapors that are created while you are pumping. All hoses at the pump have a vapor return. If you are pumping on the fast rate, some of the liquid that goes to your tank becomes vapor. Those vapors are being sucked up and back into the underground storage tank, and you're getting less gas for your money.

3. One of the most important tips is to fill up when your gas tank is HALF FULL. This is because the more gas you have in your tank the less air is occupying its empty space. Gasoline evaporates faster than you can imagine. Gasoline storage tanks have an internal floating roof that serves as zero clearance between the gas and the atmosphere to minimize evaporation.

4. One last reminder: if there is a gasoline truck pumping into the storage tanks when you stop to buy gas, DO NOT fill up! Most likely the gasoline is being stirred up as the gas is being delivered, and you might pick up some of the dirt that normally settles on the bottom of the tanks.

Parting words from the author

Well, we are at the end of our road trip. I know we traveled some roads you have never been down before. I also know for some of you there were some unexpected turns and scares. These are all good things. Going down new roads and facing fear is how we truly grow.

I designed this book so it will fit in your glove box or center console. Please keep it handy, and it will continue to help and serve you for the rest of your journey down the road. As long as they keep giving you a driver's license, vehicles will be part of your life. My goal is to help you save money during your entire trip.

There is nothing like the great sense of freedom you get on a road trip. So roll down the window, let the wind blow through your hair, turn up the radio and enjoy the ride! I look forward to seeing you out there on the road somewhere....

Louie Sharp

APPENDIX

HANDY CHECKLISTS
AND WORKSHEET

What To Do At The Scene Of An Accident

- Check for injuries in all vehicles involved and call 911 for help if needed

- Call the police - ALWAYS if you haven't already done so

- Do not move your vehicle until instructed by a Police Officer

- Get an accident report or incident report completed by Police

- Determine if your vehicle is safe to drive. When in doubt have it towed.

- Contact the correct insurance company as soon as appropriate

- Remember you have the right to choose the shop that repairs your vehicle.

KEEP ME IN YOUR GLOVE-BOX!
Visit www.louiesharp.com to download this handy form.

How To Determine When It Is Safe To Drive A Damaged Vehicle, or Not.

- Are any of the tires damaged?
- Does any part of the car touch a tire?
- Are there any fluids leaking?
- If in doubt, call a tow truck.

Should I File A Claim Calculator

Which is better for your financial situation? Note: The cost of repairs is subject to hidden damage costs if the vehicle has not been disassembled for an accurate one-time estimate. Visit www.louiesharp.com to download the full size version of this form.

1.	Cost of repair	$ 2,000		$_____
2.	Less deductible minus	- 250		- $_____
3.	Amount insurance will pay	= $ 1,750		= $_____
4.	Annual Insurance premium	$ 1,200		$_____
5.	Potential rate increase times x %	10%	times x	_____%
6.	# of years for increase times x	3	times x	_____
7.	Total rate increase equals	$ 360	equals =	$_____
8.	Out of pocket if no claim filed	$ 2,000		$_____
9.	Out of pocket if claim filed	$ 250		$_____ (deductible)
10.	Cost of rate increase (Line 7) plus	$ 360		$_____
11.	Total cost to file claim equals	$ 610		$_____

Cashing Out

The true cost to you when you cash the insurance check and don't repair the vehicle

Many insurance adjustors often write claims for 25%-30% less than the amount needed for a quality repair and offer the customer a check for that amount up front. If you use the check for repairs, you may have to sacrifice quality to complete the job. If you choose to cash the check and NOT do the repair, you still have a damaged and devalued vehicle. However, the insurance company just saved 25%-30%.

Example For Your Vehicle

1. Average claim in dollars $ 2,300 $_____

2. 25% of repair cost plus $ 575 $_____

Total amount lost equals $ 2,875 $_____

At some point you will lose $2,875 on the value of your car, either at trade-in or when you sell it outright.

The total amount lost will never go down even though the vehicle continues to depreciate.

Visit www.louiesharp.com to download a full size version of the *CASHING OUT* form.

ABOUT THE AUTHOR

Louie Sharp is wired to help people. He's been serving others non-stop since the 1970's when he served us all in the United States Marine Corps. Even after his release, Louie continued in the Marine Reserves for another sixteen years where he was a jet engine mechanic, crew chief and door gunner on both "E" and "N" model Huey helicopters.

After active duty, the automotive world seemed to be calling his name. So in 1980 Louie became a full time apprentice body man with Scott's Auto Body in Arlington Heights, Illinois. At the same time he took the first step toward owning his own shop by working nights and weekends in Island Lake, Illinois. In 1981 Sharp Auto Body opened its doors, and the dream was a reality.

By the late 80's Louie was ready for another challenge and opened his towing business where he continues to offer 24 hour towing service. In 2000, with only two businesses to run, he bought Amrich's Auto Repair in Island Lake which then became Sharp Auto and Truck Repair.

Louie Sharp is committed to excellence and well-being in everything he does. Safety, integrity and outrageous customer service are the keys to his success. I-Car certified, he is a graduate of the Automotive Management Success Program. He is an active member of the Automotive Service Association as well as DuPont's Performance

Alliance and 20 Group Programs.

Always happy to give back to the community, Louie donates his time to present his **Car Cents Program** to local high schools, community organizations and driving schools.

"LOUIE SHARP'S CAR CENTS"   Book Order Form

NAME _____

ADDRESS _____

ADDRESS _____

CITY _____

STATE _____ ZIP _____

TELEPHONE _____

EMAIL _____

SEND _____ Copies @ $ _____ Each
Add $3.00 per book for shipping, handling and applicable taxes.
Actual weight varies when ordering multiple copies and costs may
increase or decrease slightly. All orders are verified prior to ship.

TOTAL AMOUNT ENCLOSED $_____

_____

MC V DISCOVER #

EXP DATE_____ SECURITY CODE _____

_____

SIGNATURE

Mail Your Orders To: **LOUIE SHARP'S CAR CENTS**
227 WEST STATE ROAD
ISLAND LAKE, IL 60042

Email Orders To: **book@louiesharp.com**

Phone Orders Call: **847-526-1343**   **Thank You!**

Made in the USA
Middletown, DE
08 March 2023